JOURNEYING:
A BEGINNER'S GUIDE
TO THE BIBLE

For Dad
who faithfully continues the journey

JOURNEYING

A BEGINNER'S GUIDE
TO THE BIBLE

Michael Trainor

ST PAULS

JOURNEYING: a beginner's guide to the Bible
© Michael Trainor 2005

First published in 2005.

North American edition published by
Alba House, 2187 Victory Blvd,
Staten Island NY 10314-6603
www.alba-house.com
ISBN 0-8189-0986-2

UK-Ireland edition published by
ST PAULS Publishing
187 Battersea Bridge Road, London, SW11 3AS, UK
www.stpauls.ie
ISBN 085439 700 0

Australian editon published by
ST PAULS PUBLICATIONS - Society of St Paul
60-70 Broughton Road — PO Box 906— Strathfield, NSW 2135
www.stpauls.com.au

National Library of Australia
Cataloguing-in-Publication Data:
Trainor, Michael.
Journeying : a beginner's guide to the Bible
Bibliography.
ISBN 1 876295 90 2
1. Bible - Introductions. I. Title.
220.61

Cover design: Kylie Pratts
Cover Image: Good Shepherd (3rd Century CE), Vatican Museum.
Photo: Michael Trainor

Printed by Ligare Pty Ltd

ST PAULS PUBLICATIONS is an activity of the priests and brothers of the Society of St Paul who place at the centre of their lives the mission of evangelisation through the modern means of social communication.

Contents

Acknowledgments

Portions of this book were published in the author's previous work, *Befriending the Text* (Collins Dove, 1991). All material has been revised for inclusion in this book.

Chapter 1

Beginning the Journey

In my younger years I had heard and been taught that the Bible was important for the life of a Christian. My first attempt to read the Bible, however, ended in disaster. I tried to approach it like any other book, and naturally from the beginning. I began with the Book of *Genesis* and its first chapter. Not much time passed before I quietly closed the book, frustrated and disappointed. The style of writing, its language and imagery confused me. Its world seemed so different from my own, its literature so alien. This initial attempt created a feeling of distance between myself and the world of the Bible. I realised that if I were to read the Bible again I would need help. Two questions needed to be answered: How do I read such ancient literature? Where do I begin? This little book is a response to those two questions. It is an attempt to address that feeling of alienation that sometimes rises up in keen and beginning readers of the Bible.

The Bible is a library. Like any library, the Bible contains all kinds of literature written over a long period of time. This library is very old. Its earliest piece of literature was composed over 3200 years ago. It took another 1300 years for the final piece to be completed, and a further few hundred years before all these various types of writing were brought together into the Bible we have today. All these writings come from a different time and world. Their styles of writing, images and turns of phrase are quite unfamiliar. Though our Bible is in English, its original languages were Hebrew and Greek.

The venture into an initial reading of the Bible could be compared to travelling with someone that we would like to befriend. We know that our journey is very important. We have heard that our travelling companion is very gracious and friendly and has made a difference to many people's lives. We also know that our companion has often been misunderstood or misquoted. We start out on this journey tentatively, perhaps a little apprehensively, though with a desire to become friends.

It is impossible to give a comprehensive introduction to the literature of the Bible in such a small book. Far more thorough treatments will be listed at the end. Here I offer a beginners' guide for the journey, for reading the various types of literature gathered together in the biblical library. In the next few chapters I offer a few suggestions about approaching the Bible and look at some of the methods that have been used to read it. The central chapters will focus on the Bible's different types of literature. Their appreciation might help the journey and provide a way of reading. A brief description of the literary form will be offered. A suggestion for understanding the central message contained within the particular style of biblical literature will also be offered. The message or insight by the biblical writer might become the focus for discussion and provide the means for journeying further with the Bible. Finally, at least one example drawn from the Bible of the particular literary form under discussion accompanies each chapter. At the end of each chapter questions are suggested for personal or group use. These might be the focus of a parish discussion or helpful to a Bible study group.

As we prepare for the journey, I offer one final suggestion: purchase or get hold of a recent English translation of the Bible. I would recommend the *New Revised Standard Version* (for reasons that I will expand on at the end of this book). Make this Bible your own; allow yourself to mark it and write in its margins.

If this guide is used with a small group, the following might be helpful:

* Ensure that you have a recent English translation of the Bible.

* Meet, having already read the chapter of this book under discussion, the Bible texts and the questions at the end of each chapter. These questions are the focus of the meeting.

* Decide how long to meet, perhaps an hour to an hour and half. You might even think of combining a couple of the chapters for the one meeting.

* Nominate a chair or co-ordinator. This person might be different for each meeting. The chair's task is simply to ensure that all get the opportunity to speak, and to gently quieten the most talkative and opinionated, while encouraging responses from quieter members.

* Begin the meeting with a brief prayer, calling on God's Spirit to be present and to open the hearts of all to the insights in this biblical journey.

* Use questions to encourage group reflection. For example: What were people's reactions to the reading? What surprised them? What was encouraging? What was a new insight? What was difficult?

* In the last ten minutes before the end of the meeting, encourage group members to reflect on what has emerged for them. This becomes a moment for each person to name their experience of what has happened. It is not a time to go over the content or materials contained in the chapter or discuss other points of biblical interest.

* Conclude the meeting with a brief prayer of thanksgiving and the Lord's Prayer.

* Keep refreshments simple.

For personal reflection or group study

1. What is your experience of journeying with the Bible?

2. What have you found helpful in this journey?

3. What has been unhelpful?

Chapter 2

Guides for the Journey

This book will introduce the different types of literature that compose the Bible. This is not the only way of approaching a biblical text. There are so many other ways of reading the Bible, which people have used, and scholars have developed. Here we focus on one—understanding the different styles that Bible writers used.

Bible educators remind us that it is necessary to understand the cultural and social world in which each text was written. This helps us appreciate the meaning intended by the author of the biblical text for the people to whom it was first addressed. The Bible was written for a Mediterranean society, in Hebrew and Greek. This recognition is a reminder that the Bible's first audiences were not English-speaking Westerners, and their cultural values were different from our own. An appreciation of the Mediterranean understanding of honour and shame, the role of the kinship group, its perspective about time, human nature and the spirit world can assist us in our journey with the Bible. They can help us read with fresh eyes.

Besides a more culturally sensitive Bible reading, other considerations of a more literary nature can be very helpful. For example, understanding the structure of each particular work offers a clue to the author's intention. This literary context helps to situate each particular text within the overall plan, discussion or teaching of the biblical book. Awareness of Hebrew and Greek as the Bible's original languages is also a reminder that our English translations are limited and imperfect, though some are better than others. Suggestions about English translations will be found in the final chapter.

An appreciation of the way a story is developed, the plot narrated and its characters interact are further clues to a text's meaning. How passages have been referred to in other parts of the Bible or celebrated in liturgy by Christian communities over the centuries may provide further hints to their interpretation. All these approaches to reading the Bible sensitive to the cultural, textual, literary and liturgical setting have proved to be helpful for first-time readers. Bible scholars have explored more fully how these methods can assist. All these, and many others that I have not mentioned, are different but related methods that scholars have used to help readers understand the Bible.

In 1943, Pope Pius XII wrote a groundbreaking encyclical entitled *Divino Afflante Spiritu* ('Under the Inspiration of the Holy Spirit'). He acknowledged that a proper understanding of the Bible required an appreciation of its different literary forms and the time and culture of its writers. The insight of Pius XII was endorsed and expanded in the teaching of the Second Vatican Council, especially in its 1965 declaration, *Dei Verbum* ('The Word of God'). This statement affirmed the revelatory nature of the Word of God in history in human form, the centrality of the Bible to the life of the Church and the importance of the Catholic Community in reclaiming the Bible in its faith and worship life. The year before the proclamation of *Dei Verbum*, the Pontifical Biblical Commission (established in 1902 by Pope Leo XIII to assist the teaching office of the Catholic Church) issued an 'Instruction on the Historical Truth of the Gospels.' This document encouraged the use of modern methods of biblical interpretation for understanding the Gospels. In 1993, the Pontifical Biblical Commission issued another statement, significant for its endorsement of contemporary methods of biblical interpretation. The document, 'The Interpretation of the Bible in the Church', also seriously questioned a literalist approach to understanding the Bible. More about fundamentalism will be said later. Here it is important to note that an official statement of the Catholic Church acknowledges for the first time the limitations and dangers inherent in a fundamentalist reading of the Bible.

In recent decades great advances have been made in our appreciation of the Bible. The ecumenical movement with its rich collaboration between Protestant and Catholic scholars, the teachings of Vatican II, and the renewal of the liturgy and our worship life and its restoration of the centrality of the Liturgy of the Word — all have contributed to this appreciation. A huge gap still exists between biblical research and the official teaching of the Church, on the one hand, and the biblical literacy of ordinary, committed Christians, on the other. The following chapters might help to bridge that gap as we focus on the variety of literary forms found in the Bible.

For personal reflection or group study

1. What is your memory of Scripture in your parish community?

2. What has been your experience of the major changes in the place of the Bible in your worship community?

3. How is the Bible now proclaimed and reflected upon in this setting?

Chapter 3

Popular Approaches
for the Journey

Over the centuries, Christians have developed five approaches to journeying with the Bible and seeing its relevance for life. Each has its strengths and weaknesses. These approaches I call the avoidance, blueprint, proof-text, kernel and conversational approaches. I shall leave a consideration of the conversational approach to the next chapter and briefly introduce the other four here.

The *avoidance* approach is not really an approach to reading the Bible, though it is one that is very familiar to us. It is an attitude found among Christians who see the Bible as having no relevance to them. The Bible is considered as coming from a world so different from our own, that it requires complicated techniques to understand it and apply its teaching to our contemporary situation. The difficulty of reading the Bible and understanding its world leads many Christians to avoid it or to deny its centrality to Christian living.

The *blueprint* approach is what is referred to earlier as fundamentalism. It is very common. In this approach, the reader presumes that the Bible was written purposely to be understood exactly as written by today's readers. What is written is literally true and offers a divine blueprint for life. All that remains is to take the words of the Bible literally and apply them to the present situation. By 'decoding' the biblical truth that God has made plain in the pages of the Bible, the reader can know exactly what God expects of people today. This approach can appear easy and uncomplicated. Its limitation is that it does not respect the world, culture, or intent of each biblical writer.

An example of this approach would be to understand from the book of *Genesis* that God created the universe in literally six days. More about this approach will be said in chapter 15.

The *proof-text* approach is frequently used by Christians who are looking for support from the Bible for a wide range of beliefs and practices: from understanding why we do what we do, to ethical teaching and church practices. To achieve this support, a variety of texts from the Bible are gathered together on a particular topic or theme and presented. This 'proof text' approach affirms the importance of the Bible in developing authentic Church teaching. Its limitation is that it does not make allowances for the variety of writings in the Bible or respect their cultural and historical contexts. The other difficulty is that it is impossible to arrive at a unified understanding or teaching across the whole spectrum of biblical writings. What is said in one part of the Bible can be contradicted in another. To take a simple example, in the Gospels of Matthew, Mark and Luke, Simon of Cyrene helps Jesus carry his cross to Golgotha. In John's Gospel, Jesus carries the cross himself. While this particular example does not bear on church teaching, it does illustrate that texts can contradict each other, especially when taken out of context and without appreciation of what each author is attempting to teach.

The *kernel* approach is one that is used by many Bible scholars. This method presumes that by using certain techniques of biblical interpretation the correct meaning intended by the author can be deduced from the biblical text. This extracted meaning is considered the real kernel of biblical truth. It can then be the subject of reflection and application for preaching, teaching and official Church documents. The advantage of this approach is that it respects the methods of contemporary biblical scholarship, especially considering the Bible's cultural, textual, literary and liturgical contexts. Its limitation is that it can regard the world of the reader or interpreter as unimportant or, at least, secondary. An example of this kernel approach is to interpret the story of Noah in *Genesis* as a story written by an ancient writer to help the audience reflect on God's overriding concern for them. God is interpreted through this story as a God wanting to deliver the original audience from evil. This interpretation, though helpful, needs to take one more step. It needs to answer the question: What are the implications of this story for today's reader?

 For personal reflection or group study

1. From the different approaches named above, which one appeals to you?

2. What approach seems the most usual amongst the Christians you know?

Chapter 4

Conversing on the Journey

Time on a journey seems to pass much more quickly and pleasantly when we are able to have a meaningful conversation with our companion. As we talk together, we let each other know about who we are, what concerns us, what our hopes are. Companions reveal themselves to each other. Each person through their conversation adds something to the journey. All this provides us with a metaphor for thinking about a final approach in journeying with the Bible. It is what I call the 'conversational approach.'

As already indicated, the reader who wants to appreciate the Bible must respect the uniqueness of each biblical passage. This means trying to understand the time and culture in which a particular text was written and the literary context in which the passage is found in the Bible. And as we shall see, this means appreciating the type of literature which the text represents. These together allow us to understand the world of the Bible and to 'hear' the biblical text from its own setting. In this aspect of the conversational journey, the Bible is taken seriously.

Friendship is never one way and conversation is a backwards and forwards dynamic. It is mutual. Friendship occurs when there is honest, open sharing from both sides. So it is with the Bible. We converse with the Bible. We allow the Bible to speak to us. As conversation partners, neither of us is silent nor is there a monologue with the interests and context of the other forgotten. We bring our uniqueness, our story, our 'text' to the conversation. This is the dialogue. Our engagement in this biblical dynamic must also allow our voices to be heard. The Bible must allow us to speak. Likewise, our interests and perspectives should not deafen us to the voice of the Bible and its world.

How might we do this?

It is important, indeed necessary, before and during each conversation with the biblical text that we spend a moment acknowledging our inner world. We do not simply suspend our questions or life experiences until our reading or study of the Bible is over, and then take up life again as though our life and our reading of the Bible were divorced from each other. Helda Camara, formerly the Catholic Bishop of Recife, Brazil, once said that he always prayed with the Bible in one hand and the newspaper in the other. What he was referring to was the part his own concerns and experiences bring to his prayerful reflection on the Bible. As I journey with the Bible, my life concerns must be part of that journey.

* What experiences do I bring to this journey with the Bible?
* What is my story?
* What questions do I have?
* What are my social, global, church, family or personal concerns?
* What do I presently feel?
* What is going on in my life at the present?

These questions help to acknowledge ourselves as indispensable conversation partners as we journey with the Bible. During the actual reading of the text other questions might be helpful for the ongoing dialogue which we have with it:

* What do I notice in the biblical text as I read it?

* How do I feel about the text?
* What surprises, shocks or comforts me?
* What questions does the text raise in me?

Our understanding of a particular biblical text arises out of the encounter between two worlds — our world as readers and the world that has produced the text. All the questions above acknowledge that the friendship that grows through the journey occurs when our world meets and engages the world of the text. Our questions might sensitise us to certain dynamics or insights of the biblical text. The text might raise for us particular questions which we have never considered before. This movement backwards and forwards, between my world and that of the Bible, produces what I call a conversation. When two different worlds meet one another and they allow themselves to be touched by each other, friendship grows and the journey becomes a delight.

For personal reflection or group study

1. Look at one of the Bible readings for the Liturgy of the Word for next Sunday. Work through the questions above.

2. What do you think would be the easiest part about this conversational approach to journeying with the Bible? What would be the most difficult?

3. What has been helpful in this approach?

Chapter 5

Journeying with the Bible

When two friends decide to journey together the event is not just one of convenience, a way of getting from one point to another. While there is a practical aspect to the journey, friends will want to enjoy the experience together. The journey can help deepen bonds of friendship. Friends travel on a journey, but the journey becomes a means of friendship. They don't just 'take' a journey; the journey 'takes' them.

If we allow this image of the journey to be an image of our reading the Bible, then what the journey does to friends is similar to how the Bible affects us. We just don't read the Bible; the Bible 'reads' us. We are influenced and shaped by the insights that the Bible's different faith communities communicate to us through the centuries.

This image of journeying with the Bible also suggests something else. Our two friends above, who start out on a journey, need to know something about where they are going. Their journey is not aimless. It has a route and they need to know how they are going to travel. Background or basic information is essential to a journey. Similar information is needed in journeying with the Bible.

The kind of information that follows may seem to be taken for granted, but it is essential to acknowledge it. An understanding of the different literary forms found in the Bible will ease the journey. I am presuming, too, that the person who wants to journey with the Bible is looking for something more than just information about the text. I presume that the reader wants to deepen her or his relationship with God through this journey with the Bible. This is a person's quest for ultimate meaning.

As one searches for meaning in this biblical journey, the very reading of the Bible becomes most important. Through the ages, reading the Bible has been the source of sustenance and nourishment for women and men struggling to know God in their lives. For this reason, some religious communities have built their spirituality around Bible reading.

In order for this kind of spiritual sustenance through reading the Bible to be possible, I suggest that the particular text of the Bible be read *three* times, slowly and deliberately.

* The *first reading* is for understanding. The reader tries to comprehend what the text says. This is where an appreciation of literary form is important. Other factors, like the text's worldview, cultural and historical background, will also affect and deepen our appreciation. This book, then, is to assist in this first way of reading.

* The *second reading* honours the affective dimension of the engagement between text and reader. The second reading is for the heart. 'What do I experience?' 'What am I feeling?' 'What in the text addresses me as I am?' 'What resistance am I experiencing as I reflect on the reading?' Reading the text at this level allows the Bible to move more deeply into me; it opens me to make connections with the text; it allows the Bible to touch me in the core of my being.

* The *third reading* is to bring the reader's intellect and affectivity together. This reading brings a holism to the encounter. It offers an opportunity to return to the important moments already noticed in the engagement between text and reader. A third reading is often the

occasion when the Bible 'reads' the reader. It is the critical moment of confirmation or choice for the reader.

I have emphasised that the world of the reader is important for understanding and journeying with the Bible. I have also suggested a way of reading that lays a foundation for coming to a sense of ultimate meaning on the biblical journey. As suggested, such a reading relies on an understanding of the text, including its literary form. As we come to encounter the Bible, its different literary forms need to be identified and respected. To this task we now turn.

 For personal reflection or group study

1. Reflect on your 'usual' way of reading a Bible passage. How do you prepare yourself? What do you do?

2. Read *Ezekiel* 37:1-14, the story of the prophet's experience in a valley of dried bones. Use the approach to reading this text as suggested above.

3. What differences does this approach have from your 'usual' way?

Chapter 6

Story

One of the most consistent and general literary forms in the biblical library is the *story*. Stories occur throughout the Bible—beginning from the book of *Genesis*, the Bible's first book, with the stories about creation and Israel's ancestry with Sarah and Abraham. Stories continue in the New Testament: in the Gospels, and Luke's memories about the growth of the Christian community in *Acts of the Apostles*, to the final book of the Bible, the book of the *Apocalypse* (or *Revelation*), with the story of God's liberation of suffering saints. To call such writings 'stories' is not the same as saying that they are made up, or figments of the writer's imagination.

Stories have a plot. A plot is a narrative dynamic that has a certain tension created by the elements or characters of the story. As the story unfolds, the narrative tension gradually becomes resolved. Stories are not always history and are not intended to be taken literally. That is, they are not written to provide the reader with a stenographic or digital recording of an event or character. The stories may be based on some historical event, but their intention is not to tell history as such. Rather, the purpose of a story is to highlight an important religious truth. Bible stories are sacred stories.

We can ask the same simple questions about Bible stories as we would of any story: Where? When? Who? What? How? Why?

* What are the 'where' details of the story? Where is it set?

* When do the story's events unfold?

* Who are involved?

* What is the essential point of the story?

* How does the writer tell the story?

* Why did the writer tell the story in this particular way?

It is amazing what insights can be gained from using these questions. Let me offer one example from a reading of the story of God's call of the young lad Samuel in *1 Samuel* 3:1-11. This is found in the Old Testament (or, as some would prefer to call this part of the Bible, 'The First Testament'). Let me briefly track through each of the questions.

* *Where*? The story is set in the Temple in Jerusalem and God calls Samuel within this religious setting.

* *When*? At night and at a time in Israel's history when 'visions were rare'.

* *Who*? A young person, Samuel, and an older wise figure, Eli.

* *What*? Samuel discovers God calling him.

* *How*? Samuel discovers God's call through his attentiveness to God's voice and by consulting the community's wisdom figure.

* *Why*? In answering this question we come to the story's central message. Samuel reveals two essential qualities needed in any person of faith seeking to follow God's call in their lives: an openness to hear God and a willingness to consult the wisdom figure/s of the community. The journey with God is never intended to be solitary.

We all like stories. They engage, console, challenge and disturb us. The Bible is filled with stories. These are sacred stories that help us in our journey. An appreciation of the nature of story and some of the questions we can ask of these stories can help us deepen our appreciation of the Bible and come to something of their meaning for journey. In the next chapter I shall look at a particular form of story, the myth.

For personal reflection or group study

1. Read one of the following sacred stories in the Bible:
* *Exodus* 3:1-6 (Moses' encounter with God on Mt. Horeb);
* *Exodus* 12:1-13 (The celebration of the first Passover);
* *Exodus* 32:7-14 (Moses intercedes to remind God about being faithful);
* *Luke* 16:1-13 (The steward who acts to ensure that self-directed profit is not made from his master's debtors);
* *Luke* 19:1-10 (The rich Zacchaeus follows Jesus);
* *Mark* 1:40-45 (Jesus heals a leprous person).

2. Slowly work through the selected story using the six questions suggested above.

3. What fresh insights does this approach bring to your appreciation of the story you chose?

Chapter 7

Myth

One of the most famous examples of a sacred story is found in the book of *Genesis* 1:1-2:3 in the First Testament. This story of creation is one of the most important stories in the Bible. In fact, this story, is concerned about *the* story before all stories; it is about prehistory and the foundational truth about creation. This foundation is God. The story proposes a way of understanding the basic truths that shape our existence and experience of the world. Stories that help us do this are called *myths*. They help us understand the religious or theological truth about our existence.

Myths are not fictitious or pure inventions of the imagination. Some people become quite surprised when they hear that the Bible's creation stories or the other sacred stories in *Genesis* 1-11 are myths. They think that the stories are being described as fanciful. This is far from the truth. In the sense used here, myths communicate religious truth. They are not fictitious or fanciful for they are concerned with reality as it exists. They are symbolic stories. The total narrative enables us as readers to move through the elements of the story to the deeper reality which these elements symbolise and communicate. A preoccupation with the literal meaning of each detail of the characters or events or elements that compose the story keeps us only on the surface of the mythic story. The art of comprehending the deeper truth of the story, and so journeying with the Bible with its mythic stories, requires that we move into the story's deeper levels. This is what is intended by the writer and symbolised through the story itself.

Unfortunately, the creation story is one of the most misunderstood stories in the whole Bible. It is often interpreted not as a mythic story but literally. This is especially the case by those who hold a 'fundamentalist' point of view and use the 'blueprint' approach as discussed in chapter 3. Fundamentalists read a story without taking into account the cultural context or worldview at the time the particular text was written. They read the story of creation only from their own point of view. They understand the story of creation as an historical account of what actually happened when God created the world. They would argue that God created the universe literally in six days, in the order that the story recounts. The story is then used as an argument against any modern scientific explanation of the origins of the universe, like evolution.

A literal or blueprint reading of this story creates a wedge between theology and science. The most unfortunate aspect of such an approach is that it misses the main point that the writer wanted to communicate to the original audience. This is the theological truth or message which the story expresses.

The story of creation was borrowed from one of the many stories of creation circulating in Mesopotamian culture around the 6th century BCE. (In preference to BC and AD, more and more Bible interpreters are using 'BCE' and 'CE'. These mean 'Before the Common Era' and 'The Common Era'. The Common Era is the period of history common to both Jews and Christians. BCE is the era prior to the history shared by Jewish and Christian communities.) The story, therefore, reflected the limited, scientific worldview of the time. The religious writer reshaped the story in the light of Israel's belief in one God.

As mentioned in the previous chapter, a feature of a story is the resolution of conflict or tension. This is most evident in *Genesis* 1:1-2:3. The conflict between opposing forces (formless void/spirit, light/darkness, upper/lower waters, day/night, sun/moon, fish/birds) is resolved through God's powerful and creative word.

> The earth was a formless void and darkness covered the face of the deep, while a wind from God swept over the face of the waters. Then God said ... . (*Gen* 1:2-3a)

In the story, God creates in six days the world in which humans will live. On the seventh day, God rests. So the story is about the first week of history. It shows why the Jewish Sabbath was sanctified. The story is ultimately about God and God's care of creation, especially of humans within creation.

The story is carefully constructed and finely balanced. Out of the formless abyss and darkness, God creates. Day one is the creation of light (and day and night). On day two, God separates the water above from the water beneath. This is necessary in a worldview that saw water as primordial matter. On day three, the lower waters are separated to create land and seas. The land is adorned with plants. The celestial lights (the sun and moon) are created on day four to adorn the heavens. This leads to God's creation of living creatures (day five), animals and humans (day six). The creation of the human person on the sixth day is climactic. God creates the human 'in our image, according to our likeness'. Humans reflect God by their activity over the whole of creation and through their care of their environment. The creation of humanity leads to the final seventh day. This is the day on which God rests.

Through the story's structure, the writer firmly establishes the Jewish Sabbath within God's plan and order for creation. However, there are other important insights that this mythic story offers. These insights are the deeper religious truths symbolised through the story.

The story teaches that God is the source of all of creation. The writer emphasises that this world is fundamentally good and that humanity is a unique reflection of the activity and image of God. This is highlighted at the end of each creation day when the writer says 'And God saw that it was good.' When God looked at everything created, including the human being, we read that 'indeed, it was very good' (*Gen* 1:31).

The story of creation in *Genesis* 1 is, of course, another among the vast library of sacred stories in the Bible. As a mythic story it beautifully communicates a theology about God, creation and humanity. It also demonstrates how the biblical story is not concerned with making points about science or history. The essence of the biblical story, rather, is its communication of religious truth. It helps the reader become oriented to God and to make the connections between the world of human experience and God's presence within this world. The mythic story assists in the reader's discovery of meaning.

For personal reflection or group study

1. Read one of the following mythic stories in the Bible:
* *Genesis* 2:4-7 (A second creation story);
* *Genesis* 2:18-25 (God's creation of human companionship);
* *Genesis* 3:1-7 (The human desire to be as God);
* *Genesis* 3:8-21 (The humans seek to blame each other and avoid God);
* *Genesis* 4:8-16 (A brother kills his sibling);
* *Genesis* 8:1-22 (God liberates Noah).

2. Slowly read the selected story in the light of this chapter and an appreciation of the biblical myth.

3. What fresh insights does this appreciation bring to your reading?

Chapter 8

The Epic

A type of biblical story concerned with salvific events, or people of heroic character, is the *epic*. Stories about Abraham, Sarah, Moses, Joseph and Joshua in *Genesis* and *Exodus*, are examples of the epic. Over time, with continual reflection by the community, these events, heroes and heroines assume impressive proportions in the minds of the members of the religious community. Every time they are spoken about in this community, new insights and deeper levels of appreciation develop. They become larger than life and the centrepiece of the epic.

The story of Moses and the Exodus in the Book of *Exodus* is the classic epic in the First Testament. Every other event in the salvific history of the Hebrew people is dwarfed by the *Exodus* account.

The great act of liberation itself is described in *Exodus* 14. This epic, written in the 6th century BCE, describes an event that occurred around 1300 BCE. In the telling and retelling of the story over the eight centuries before the story came into its present, final form, the significance of the event and Moses' role for the life of Israel became more obvious. Both assumed an important and central place in the story of Israel.

Whether the event originally involved a great number of Hebrews (more than 600, 000, if we take *Exodus* 12:37 literally) or whether it involved a motley collection of runaway slaves is not as important as the theological message. In time the actual historical details of the epic gave way to the theological truth evident in *Exodus* 14:30-31:

> Thus the Lord saved Israel that day from the Egyptians; and Israel saw the Egyptians dead on the seashore. Israel saw the great work that the Lord did against the Egyptians. So the people feared the Lord and believed in the Lord and in his servant Moses.

The *Exodus* epic, like so many other epics in the Bible, spelt out the place of God in Israel's story. God was regarded as the agent of Israel's liberation. It was God who saved Israel from potential annihilation by a great and powerful foreign army. The Exodus was ultimately God's act of love for Israel.

The *Exodus* epic cannot be told without linking it to the other dominant epic in Israelite history, the covenant which God formed with the Hebrew people through Moses on Mount Sinai (*Ex* 20). These two events, the Exodus and the Sinai covenant, were the two great formative events in Israel's history. Every other experience in history was judged in the light of these two. They shaped the way the Hebrew people saw themselves and their relationship with God. These two epics produced reverential awe (unfortunately, often translated as 'fear') in the hearts of the Israelites.

A final point about the *Exodus* epic is its connection to the creation story. The Exodus was a prototype for so many other stories in the First Testament and may have even shaped the way the creation story was written. The emphasis on God bringing order out of chaos and the furnishing of creation through the act of 'separation' are themes central to both stories. In both, God separates the water to provide dry land. The Exodus could also be interpreted as a new creative act of God for the Hebrew people that became formalised in the Sinai covenant.

For personal reflection or group study

1. Read one of the following epics in the Bible:
* *Genesis* 12:1-9 (God calls Abram to leave his homeland);
* *Genesis* 17:1-22 (God makes a covenant with Abram);
* *Genesis* 16:1-16 (The tension in Abram's family);
* *Genesis* 22:1-19 (Abraham — earlier called 'Abram' — undertakes an ultimate test of faith);
* *Genesis* 37:1-36 (Joseph is betrayed by his brothers and sold into slavery);
* *Exodus* 20:1-26 (God makes a covenant with the Israelites through Moses).

2. Slowly read the selected story in the light of this chapter and an appreciation of the Bible's epics.

3. What fresh insights does this appreciation bring to the reading of your chosen epic?

Chapter 9

History

We have a fascination and a preoccupation with history. Our understanding has been influenced by a nineteenth century approach to history. We like to know all the details and facts of an event. In a world that seems very fragile and unstable, connection with our historical roots can provide a sense of identity and purpose before an unknown future.

The Bible also shows a concern for history and offers the reader several examples of historical writing. For example, in the First Testament we see eyewitness accounts of court history in the first and second books of *Samuel* and the first and second books of *Kings*, stylised court history in the first and second books of *Chronicles* and the first and second books of *Kings*, epic history in *Exodus* and even prehistory in *Genesis*. In the writings of the Christian era which are part of the Bible (usually known as 'The New Testament' but which I prefer to call 'The Second Testament'), the *Gospels according to Matthew, Mark, Luke* and *John* and the *Acts of the Apostles* can be understood broadly as forms of biblical history. (We shall discuss the specific literary form of the Gospels later).

The history writers of the Bible were, however, not obsessed by our fastidiousness for historical details. The Bible's record of past events differs from the way the modern historiographer would write about these events. Our concern is with accuracy; the Bible's was with meaning.

Bible authors were not concerned with the accuracy of recorded information but with the theological significance of past events for present and future generations. From this perspective, there is a connection between modern and biblical history. Both stem from a desire to allow past events affect the present and future. The difference lies in the attitude to past events.

For the contemporary historian, the past is recorded and the events of history allowed to speak for themselves. The implications of these events are left to the interpretation of the reader. Though even with this there is an aspect of interpretation. No one writes 'objective' history. Events are remembered and recorded for a purpose. In biblical history, events of the past are deliberately and explicitly interpreted. This interpretation of history comes from the writer's faith perspective.

The biblical historian can be considered more like a 'theologian'. A theologian is one who enables the faith community to understand its present experiences in the light of its received heritage of beliefs and sacred wisdom. The biblical historian, like the theologian, interprets for the present generation those events of history that have affected the life of the present faith community. The historian-theologian reflects on these events in the light of the bond which exists between God and the believing community. The historian is concerned with writing a theological history. History is told for a purpose; facts or events are recorded with a particular theological purpose in mind.

The historical narrative in chapter 6 of the *Acts of the Apostles* in the Second Testament can be cited as an example of this form of theological history. The writer of *Acts* is the same person who wrote the *Gospel according to Luke*. This second work was probably written around the mid eighties of the first century (CE) during a time of intense missionary activity. Luke sought to offer a way of reflecting on the growth of the Christian community and for dealing with serious pastoral issues.

The story in *Acts* 6:1-7 describes a conflict in the early Christian community at Jerusalem between the Greek-speaking Christians and the Hebrew-speaking Christians. The pastoral ministers within the community were overlooking this latter group. In an assembly of all its members, the leaders of the community decided to appoint seven who would look after those in need. The main purpose of this new pastoral and administrative structure was to ensure the faithful preaching of the Word of God:

> Now during these days, when the disciples were increasing in number, the Hellenists complained against the Hebrews because their widows were being neglected in the daily distribution of food. And the twelve called together the whole community of the disciples and said, 'It is not right that we should neglect the word of God in order to wait on tables. Therefore, friends, select from among yourselves seven men of good standing, full of the Spirit and of wisdom, whom we may appoint to this task, while we, for our part will devote ourselves to prayer and to serving the word.' What they said pleased the whole community, and they chose Stephen, a man full of faith and the Holy Spirit, together with Philip, Prochorus, Nicanor, Timon, Parmenas, and Nicolaus, a proselyte of Antioch. They had these men stand before the apostles, who prayed and laid their hands on them.

> And the word of God continued to spread; the number of the disciples increased greatly in Jerusalem, and a great many of the priests became obedient to the faith.

Luke recounted an event of the past. Whether the event took place in exactly the way Luke wrote it was not a central concern. The story was told to illustrate the necessity of outreach to the community's most needy, the importance of flexible structures to attend to the pastoral needs as these surfaced within the community, and the centrality of the Word of God for community life. This is demonstrated in the way the story is written and structured around the statement '... we ... will devote ourselves to prayer and to serving the word.'

Luke illustrates the way biblical history is recounted from a theological perspective to nourish the faith life of a community of believers as it ministers in the present and prepares for its future.

 For personal reflection or group study

1. Read one of the following theological histories in the Bible:

* *Joshua* 3:14-17 (God's people crosses through the Jordan river to the Promised Land);
* *Joshua* 6:1-21 (Jericho is captured);
* *Judges* 6:11-24 (God calls a timid but potentially strong leader, Gideon, for Israel);
* *Judges* 13:2-25 (The birth of Samson);
* *1 Samuel* 17:38-51 (The boy, David, defeats the Philistine hero, Goliath);
* *Acts* 3:1-10 (Peter heals a man lame from birth).

2. Slowly read the selected story in the light of this chapter and an appreciation of the Bible's theological history.

3. What fresh insights does this appreciation bring to your reading?

Chapter 10

Poetry and Song

Poetry is a prominent literary form in almost every book of the Bible. Examples of it can be identified in the first five books of the Bible (called the 'Pentateuch'), the Book of *Psalms* (also called the 'Psalter'), the *Song of Solomon*, *Proverbs*, *Sirach*, *Wisdom* and *Job*. In the Second Testament it is evident in the canticles in *Luke* 1-2 and the early Christian hymns in *Philippians*, *Romans*, *Colossians*, *Ephesians*, *Hebrews*, and the *Apocalypse* (*Revelation*).

Since the first years of the Bible's writing, poetry has always been used to express the inner movement and intuition of the human spirit and the perception of God's involvement in human affairs.

The oldest piece of biblical poetry is Miriam's song in *Exodus* 15:1-19. Probably composed around the 12th century BCE, it is a song of thanksgiving which recounts in poetic form Israel's victory over Egypt through the power of God.

> I will sing to the Lord, for he has triumphed gloriously;
> horse and rider he has thrown into the sea. (*Ex* 15:1)

The song is addressed to God who is worshipped as strong and powerful. The song's images for God are drawn out of the author's perception of God's defeat of the evil that surrounds Israel. This evil is symbolised in the warring nation of Egypt. The song concludes with both Israel's possession of the 'holy mountain' where the people will worship God and a confident note of God's continuing reign.

> You brought them in and planted them on the mountain of
> your possession,
> the place, O Lord, that you made your abode,
> the sanctuary, O Lord, that your hands have established.
> The Lord will reign forever and ever. (*Ex* 15:17-18)

The book of *Psalms* is filled with poetry. Its various hymns are about praise, sorrow, wisdom, royalty, liturgy and history. The songs of sorrow or lament are the most common type of psalms in the Psalter. They seek God's help in time of national or personal tragedy.

Psalm 102 is a fine example of the lament song. It is the cry for help from someone who is seriously ill.

> Hear my prayer, O Lord;
> let my cry come to you.
> Do not hide your face from me
> in the day of my distress.
> Incline your ear to me;
> answer me speedily in the day when I call. (*Ps* 102:1-2)

The suffering of the person is vividly described by the poet:

> ... my bones burn like a furnace.
> My heart is stricken and withered like grass;
> I am too wasted to eat my bread. (*Ps* 102:3-4)

The song poignantly emphasises the loneliness of the sick person who seems 'like an owl of the wilderness, like a little owl of the waste places. ... like a lonely bird on the housetop' (vs 6-7). Suffering forces the sick person to realise the fragility and transitoriness of human existence.

Despite the experience of suffering and isolation, the one who prays the song seeks the God of Israel's history. In spite of the shortness of human life, the suffering person knows that God has pitied the exiled and suffering people of Israel. This recollection enables the poet to conclude the lament with a note of hope—the children of God's servants will 'live secure'.

The whole song, typical of the psalms of lament, seeks God within the context of human suffering. It faithfully acknowledges that God is not divorced from the human predicament. God does not fail to attend to the afflictions of either the individual or the nation.

A third example of poetry in song is found in the *Song of Solomon* (sometimes called the *Song of Songs* or the *Canticle of Canticles*). Here the sensual attraction between two lovers is celebrated.

> Let him kiss me
> with the kisses of his mouth!
> For your love is better than wine,
> your anointing oils are fragrant,
> your name is perfume poured out ... (1:2-3)

Jewish and Christian communities have always maintained that the eight chapters of the *Song of Solomon* are essential to the biblical collection. That this ancient song is part of the Bible underscores human love and sexuality as appropriate symbols of divine love. God's own passion for humankind is mirrored in the passion of two lovers for one another. Such an appreciation counteracts an attitude that denigrates human sexuality and the body.

The above examples of biblical poetry by no means exhaust all the variety of poetry that the Bible contains. Such a poetic spectrum, assortment of themes and range of human emotions celebrated in song, reinforce a central conviction to the person of faith. No thing, no event, no human emotion nor experience is unworthy of God's self-communication.

From Miriam's jubilant song over Israel's victory in *Exodus* 15, to the tragic psalms of lament in the book of *Psalms*, or the passionate and sensual lyrics in the *Song of Solomon*, every human experience can potentially reveal aspects of God's nature and graciousness.

These songs reflect the biblical poets' confidence in a God intimately involved in human affairs. Poetry was part of a biblical tradition that appreciated the inter-connection between the divine and the human. Our modern tendency to limit the divine to the realm of the supernatural was not shared by the ancient Israelites. The biblical poets and songwriters regarded every human activity and sentiment as being under the auspices of God. Everything was a reflection of God and guided by God. Biblical poetry and hymns were born out of this deep theological conviction.

 For personal reflection or group study

1. Read one of the following hymns or poems in the Bible:
* *Psalm* 18 (God's response to one in deep distress);
* *Psalm* 23 (In praise of God as a shepherd);
* *Psalm* 150 (The final psalm in the Psalter and one which praises God);
* *Philippians* 2:5-11 (A hymn about Jesus);
* *Colossians* 1:15-20 (A hymn about Jesus as the cosmic power);
* *1 Timothy* 3:16 (A short hymn about Jesus).

2. Slowly read the selected text in the light of this chapter and an appreciation of Bible hymns or poems.

3. What fresh insights does this appreciation bring to the Bible hymn or poem you have chosen?

Chapter 11

Wisdom

All of us seek wisdom. We want to know how to live; we continually look for answers to some of the most complex riddles of human existence; we seek to pass on to others the things that matter to us most in life; we would like to communicate our skills or gifts in a way that would benefit others. All these aspects of human living are concerned with wisdom. They are the basis for a body of writing in the Bible called 'wisdom' literature.

In the Ancient Near East, wisdom was highly sought after:

> Happy are those who find wisdom,
> and those who get understanding,
> for her income is better than silver,
> and her revenue better than gold.
> She is more precious than jewels,
> and nothing you desire can compare with her.
>
> *(Prov* 3:13-15)

Wisdom is a broad term. It is more than intellectual knowledge. It includes the skill of an artisan, perception and intuition, piety, the proper way to live, and how to survive in life:

> Do not plan harm against your neighbour
> who lives trustingly beside you.
> Do not quarrel with anyone without cause,
> when no harm has been done to you.
> Do not envy the violent
> and do not choose any of their ways. *(Prov* 3:29-31)

Besides the book of *Proverbs*, wisdom literature is found in *Sirach*, *Ecclesiastes*, *Job* and the book of *Wisdom*.

The reason that wisdom literature, including reflections on secular wisdom, was included in the Bible is similar to what we have already identified within poetry: human experience was the proper arena for God's self-revelation. The two were not divorced. That which uplifted the human spirit or expressed the fruits of human activity and passed from one generation to the next (what we would call human 'skill') was a fitting subject for reflection on the nature of God.

The book of *Wisdom* (or the *Wisdom of Solomon*) presents us with an excellent example of the wisdom literature of the Bible. Writing in the latter part of the first century BCE, the author offered encouragement and direction to fellow Jews living in Alexandria. These people experienced crisis in their Jewish faith as they attempted to live with the Hellenistic culture of this Egyptian city. Compromise and borrowing from other pagan religions had become popular ways by which the Jewish people sought to resolve the tension created between their traditional Jewish faith and practices, on the one hand, and the Greek philosophies, religions and sciences of their day, on the other.

The author borrowed from contemporary Greek culture to reassert Jewish faith and to witness to God's care for those who were faithful. This was especially evident in the writer's expectation of life after death. The writer was convinced that God rewarded those who were faithful:

> But the souls of the righteous are in the hand of God,
> and no torment will ever touch them.
> In the eyes of the foolish they seemed to have died,
> and their departure was thought to be a disaster,
> and their going from us to be their destruction;
> but they are at peace ...
> their hope is full of immortality. (*Wis* 3:1-4)

Wisdom sayings are also found in the Second Testament, particularly in the parables of Jesus. Although the parables represent a unique literary form themselves and deserve separate discussion, they are closely associated with wisdom literature and the wisdom sayings.

Although capable of a variety of definitions, the parable in essence was a surprising riddle drawn from a common experience of life which arrested the interest of the listener. The twist in the riddle, which produced the surprise, moved the listener to comprehend new dimensions of life. For this reason, the parable had the capacity to enable a receptive listener to experience God's presence (the 'reign of God') within Jesus' teaching.

In the *Gospel of Matthew*, the majority of parables are found in chapter 13. The parable of the mustard seed illustrates the wisdom character of parables and their potential as vehicles of the reign of God:

> The kingdom of heaven is like a mustard seed that someone took and sowed in his field; it is the smallest of all the seeds, but when it has grown it is the greatest of shrubs and becomes a tree, so that the birds of the air come and make nests in its branches. (*Mt* 13:31-32)

Two surprises in the parable expose listeners to the possibilities for God's reign and presence envisaged by Jesus. First, the near imperceptibility of a seed that sprouts into a tree in which birds can nest speaks of the invisible yet inherently powerful potential of God's reign. The second surprise occurs when the listener discovers that the seed becomes 'the greatest of shrubs'. The listener would have expected that the seed become a great tree, like a cedar of Lebanon. Even the humble shrub can become a symbol of God's reign.

God's reign is present in unexpected events and unrecognised characters. A woman searching for a coin, a shepherd finding a lost sheep, a hated enemy, a sower, netted fish, birds and flowers—all can communicate something of the meaning of God's presence.

The parables, like all the wisdom sayings in the First Testament, were about ordinary objects or events of life. The parables connected the listener to the real world. Through the parables, the listener actually engaged life. Ultimately, if one was receptive to the Bible's wisdom sayings, one was also receptive to God.

For personal reflection or group study

1. Read one of the following passages of wisdom from the Bible:
* *Job* 38 (God addresses Job after he makes his complaint);
* *Job* 42:1-6 (Job recognises who he is before God);
* *Psalm* 1 (A wisdom psalm);
* *Matthew* 18:1-20 (Jesus offers some wisdom to the faith community);
* *Luke* 15 (Three wisdom stories about joy over finding the lost);
* *Mark* 4:1-12 (Jesus' parable about sowing seed).

2. Slowly read the selected passage in the light of this chapter and an appreciation of wisdom writings.

3. What fresh insights does this appreciation of wisdom bring to your reading?

Chapter 12

Prophecy

All of us are prophets at one time or another. We might encourage others in a course of action that is difficult, or speak out against something we believe to be wrong, support a cause of justice, show our disagreement, go against a group's way of thinking, or propose alternative solutions to an issue or problem. All these ways of being or acting are prophetic.

An important, but misunderstood literary form in the Bible is that of *prophecy*. Prophetic literature comprises a significant portion of the First Testament and includes the writings of the classical prophets Amos, Hosea, Isaiah, Micah, Nahum, Zephaniah, Habakkuk, Jeremiah and Ezekiel. Their writings were composed between the 8th and 6th centuries BCE.

Our appreciation of biblical prophecy is clouded by our experience and use of language. For many, a prophet is only someone who foretells or predicts the future — like a fortune-teller or weather forecaster. We think that the prophet of the Bible is someone who also predicts the future, who tells the people what is going to happen to themselves or their city, or what exactly God is going to do. While there is a sense of future in biblical prophecy, this future orientation is minor or secondary. Any future orientation in biblical prophecy arises out of reflection on the present in the light of the religious tradition of the past.

Rather than thinking of the biblical prophet as a foreteller, it is more accurate to consider the prophet as a 'forth-teller.' The ordinary examples of prophecy given above are examples of this 'forth-telling.' A prophet is someone who speaks forth the implications of the people's relationship with God within their present lifestyle. The prophets knew themselves to be called by God. They were so attuned to God, knowing God's heart, that they could speak authoritatively on behalf of God.

The prophets confronted people, especially rulers and leaders in Israel, with the demands of the Covenant, which God had made with Moses on Sinai. The Covenant formalised the commitment between the Hebrew people and God. The prophets frequently called the rulers in Israel to honour this commitment. The prophet was the conscience of Israel.

An example of the prophet calling the ruler to integrity is illustrated in the story of Elijah the prophet and his critique of the Israelite king, Ahab, who ruled over Israel between the years 869 and 850 BCE. In one incident, Ahab unjustly sought to confiscate the vineyard of a poor man called Naboth. Ahab had him killed. Elijah confronted the powerful Ahab with the implications of his action:

> 'Thus says the Lord: Have you killed, and also taken possession?' ... 'I have found you. Because you have sold yourself to do what is evil in the sight of the Lord, I will bring disaster upon you; I will consume you, and will cut off from Ahab every male, bond or free, in Israel'. (1 Kings 21:19-21)

This strong prophetic word from Elijah brought Ahab to repent of the evil he had done.

Another fine example of the biblical prophet is Amos. Amos exercised his prophetic ministry during a time of material prosperity and social degradation in the 8th century BCE — like the other classical prophets, Hosea, Isaiah and Micah. From the introduction to the book of *Amos*, we know that the prophet was a farmer who looked after sheep and sycamore trees near Tekoa, in the hill country of Judah (*Amos* 1:1; 7:14).

Amos, in the style of all biblical prophets, was a 'forth-teller'. He spoke out against the injustices that were being perpetrated by the powerful within the society of Israel. He denounced wealthy landowners who took over the property of poor farmers; he berated merchants who were scrupulously careful to abstain from work on days of religious festival but who conscientiously took advantage of the poverty-stricken. The prophet spoke strongly against this form of profiteering. Such hypocrisy went against God's law:

> Hear this, you that trample on the needy,
> and bring to ruin the poor of the land,
> saying, 'When will the new moon be over
> so that we may sell grain; and the sabbath,
> so that we may offer wheat for sale?
> We will make the ephah small and the shekel great,
> and practise deceit with false balances,
> buying the poor for silver and the needy for a pair of sandals,
> and selling the refuse of the wheat. (*Amos* 8:4-6)

Amos illustrates how much the prophetic act was rooted in the present social experience of people. He reflected on the present situation in the light of the covenantal relationship between God and Israel. This enabled him to speak about the future. Society was going to collapse because it lacked justice and because the wealthy did not honour their relationship with God. This was expressed in their lack of care for the poor:

Amos was a social prophet. He reflected on the state of his own society in the light of God's law handed down from Moses. He called Israel back to fidelity to God and to justice in its dealing with all of God's people, particularly the poor:

> Seek good and not evil, that you may live;
> and so the Lord, the God of hosts, will be with you,
> just as you have said.
> Hate evil and love good, and establish justice in the gate;
> it may be that the Lord, the God of hosts,
> will be gracious to the remnant of Joseph. (*Amos* 5:14-15)

For the early Christians reflecting on the ministry of Jesus, it was not difficult to see how Jesus himself ministered like the prophets in the Hebrew Scriptures. Like Amos, Jesus was concerned for the people of his day who were disenfranchised by a social system that often favoured the wealthy. A consistent image of Jesus in the Gospels is that he called people back to the basis of religion—their relationship to God as expressed in their dealing with each other. Jesus' prophetic style was centred on justice and integrity. He called people to see again the basis of their relationship with God. His prophetic stance, calling the society of his day back to the heart of its relationship with God, illustrates how central prophecy had been in Israel. It was one important aspect of the Jewish Scriptures that shaped Jesus' own spirituality. As we shall now see, other aspects of Jesus' ministry were also captured by the earliest Christian writers in the Gospels.

For personal reflection or group study

1. Read one of the following pieces of prophetic writing from the Bible:

* *Jeremiah* 19:1-15 (The prophet acts for God to reveal Jerusalem's way of living);

* *Ezekiel* 12:17-25 (The prophet illustrates the implications of infidelity to God);

* *Amos* 6:1-7 (The prophet targets those who benefit from the exploitation of the poor);

* *Habakkuk* 1:2-3; 2:2-4 (The prophet cries to God for deliverance from violence. God offers a vision of the possible);

* *Luke* 16:19-31 (Jesus' challenge about how wealth must be used to alleviate the needs of the poor);

* *Luke* 12:13-21 (Jesus warns against a greed that forgets about what is most important).

2. Slowly read the selected passage in the light of this chapter and an appreciation of prophetic writing.

3. What fresh insights does this appreciation bring to your reading?

Chapter 13

The Gospels

For the Christian, the Gospels are considered the Bible's most important literary works; they are foundational for understanding Jesus. Since they occupy almost half of the Second Testament, the Gospels are worthy of a separate treatment. Although other literary elements involved in the Gospels, like story and parables, have already been discussed, the Gospels can also be considered a unique literary form. They offer us an insight into the way the earliest Christian communities understood Jesus and interpreted his teaching in the light of their own local situations. Simply put, a Gospel is the story of Jesus as reflected on, and told by, a community of Jesus' disciples.

The principles of biblical interpretation discussed above with regard to history and story apply also to our interpretation of the Gospels. Therefore, when we read a gospel story about Jesus we are not getting a literal retelling of an event from a 'day-in-the-life-of Jesus'. It is not a story recounted for the purpose of providing biographical information. Nor is the Gospel writer like a newspaper reporter offering the reader an account of an event historically accurate and detailed.

When we read a story in the gospel, the story itself has gone through *three stages* of development before it has reached the final form as we have it in the Bible:

* The *first stage* is the story's foundation, based in the life of Jesus himself. Each gospel event is established on the ministry of Jesus of Nazareth. In that ministry, Jesus

adapted his teaching according to the circumstances of his audience. When Jesus spoke to farmers he used images drawn from farming life. Many of his parables used images familiar to country people. The parable of the sower is an example of this. When Jesus addressed city people, his language adapted accordingly. The language he used and the deeds he performed were influenced by the audience's receptivity and locale (country or city).

* The *second stage* of the formation of the Gospel occurred when the deeds and words of Jesus became themselves the subject of the preaching of the first generation of believers. In their missionary preaching, they too adapted their preaching about Jesus according to the circumstances of their audience. For a Jewish audience Jesus was described in Jewish terms ('Son of David', 'Son of Man', 'Messiah', 'Lamb of God'). In a non-Jewish ('Gentile') setting other appropriate images were used of Jesus ('Christ', 'Word', 'King'). The way the story of Jesus was remembered was shaped by the cultural background and experiences of the audience. For example, to an audience experiencing suffering or martyrdom, Jesus' suffering was reflected upon; to a community involved in mission, Jesus' own journey and mission were highlighted in preaching.

* The *third* and final *stage* in the formation of the gospel stories occurred soon after the first preachers died. On their death, the faith communities which they established saw the need to set in writing the stories about Jesus' words and deeds which they had received from their respective founders. The Gospels came into being. The writing of each of these Gospels was shaped, as in the previous two stages, by the circumstances of the communities.

A correct understanding and interpretation of the Gospels relies on an appreciation of these three stages of gospel formation, an approach reinforced in 1964 by the

Pontifical Biblical Commission in its statement, 'Instruction on the Historical Truth of the Gospels'. Since the gospel stories have gone through three stages of development, it is easy to see that the stories as we have them in the Gospels are not historical reconstructions of events. They have been reflected on and recounted through the lens of Jesus' resurrection and the particular experiences of each of the communities. The gospel stories, then, are biased accounts. They are biased in terms of faith. When we read a gospel story, we are picking up the religious significance which a particular event or teaching has in the life of a Christian community.

The *Gospel according to Mark* was the first Gospel written. Most biblical interpreters date it around 70 CE. It was written for a mixed Gentile and Jewish Christian community, probably located in Rome and threatened with persecution.

Mark's Gospel is the shortest of the four. It begins with the preaching of John the Baptist preparing for the coming of Jesus and ends with the resurrection story. Mark portrays Jesus as the suffering one from God. He is misunderstood and rejected by the religious leaders in Israel (*Mk* 2), by his own townspeople (*Mk* 6:1-6) and even by his own family (*Mk* 3:21). The disciples, too, struggle to understand Jesus (*Mk* 8:31-33; 9:30-32; 10:32-45). The story of Jesus' death and resurrection are the climax of Mark's Gospel. Both leave the reader reflecting deeply on the person of Jesus and his presence to a struggling, misunderstood and lonely Christian community.

The limitations of this small book allow us to savour only one gospel story in depth. The one that I have chosen is the powerful and highly symbolic nature miracle in *Mark* 4:35-41:

> On that day, when evening had come, he said to them,
> 'Let us go across to the other side.' And leaving the crowd

behind, they took him with them in the boat, just as he was. Other boats were with him. A great windstorm arose, and the waves beat into the boat, so that the boat was already being swamped. But he was in the stern, asleep on the cushion; and they woke him up and said to him, 'Teacher, do you not care that we are perishing?' He woke up and rebuked the wind, and said to the sea, 'Peace! Be still!' Then the wind ceased, and there was a dead calm. He said to them, 'Why are you afraid? Have you still no faith?' And they were filled with awe and said to one another, 'Who then is this, that even the wind and the sea obey him?'.

For Mark's community members, their reflection on the story of Jesus' calming the wind and waves swamping a tiny boat would have led them to reflect on their own situation. They would have easily identified with the disciples in the boat with Jesus.

From their perspective, the constant experience of persecution and martyrdom would have left them feeling like a boat battling against wind and waves. In the midst of this suffering, they cry out to Jesus to save them lest they perish. The questions which Jesus addresses to the disciples after he has calmed an apparently overpowering storm are the same questions which are addressed to Mark's community: 'Why are you afraid? Have you no faith?'.

The experience of persecution has called into question the faith of Mark's community. The issue is not the apparent slumber of a Jesus unconcerned about the Christians' suffering; it is rather the fidelity of the disciples before life's tragedies. Once Jesus' calming presence is recognised the struggling community is left reflecting on the very nature of Jesus: 'Who then is this ... ?'.

This nature miracle in *Mark* is a story about the struggle for faith. It ends with the reader directed to the person of Jesus and provoked to think deeply about him. The way the reader is left focusing on the person of Jesus is common to all of the Gospels.

The *Gospels of Matthew* and *Luke*, probably written around 80-90 CE, are independent of each other, yet dependent on *Mark* and written in a similar vein.

Matthew was written for an audience very familiar with things Jewish. It quotes often from the First Testament and portrays Jesus as a faithful son of Israel. However, Matthew's main concern is to show Jesus as the authentic rabbinic teacher, one like the greatest teacher in Israelite history, Moses. Jesus is the Saviour sent by God. He is Emmanuel (*Mt* 1:23) — the presence of God offering salvation not only to Matthew's struggling community, but to the whole of creation. This is well illustrated in Matthew's reworking of Mark's nature miracle that we read above:

> And when he got into the boat, his disciples followed him. And behold, there arose a great storm on the sea, so that the boat was being swamped by the waves; but he was asleep. And they went and woke him, saying, 'Save us, Lord; we are perishing.' And he said to them, 'Why are you afraid, ones of little faith?' Then he rose and rebuked the winds and the sea; and there was a great calm. And human beings were in awe, saying 'What sort of person is this, that even winds and sea obey him?' (*Mt* 8:23-27. My translation)

In the story, the parts in italics are the major alterations that Matthew makes to the original story received from Mark. The Gospel writer heightens the sense of cosmic crisis (with a 'great storm on the sea' — literally, in the Greek text, 'a great earthquake'), accentuates the helplessness of the boat itself ('... the boat was being swamped by the waves') and carefully highlights the close bond between Jesus and his disciples. The disciples follow Jesus into the boat. This closeness is missing in Mark's story. Matthew also heightens Jesus' power in the face of the tempest threatening to annihilate the community of disciples (= 'boat'). Jesus is addressed as 'Lord' instead of Mark's 'Teacher'; his power leaves humanity spellbound, marvelling, 'What sort of person is this, that even winds and sea obey him?' (*Mt* 8:27).

Matthew's reworking of Mark's story has transformed a story concerned with the disciples' faith in the presence of Jesus into one that presents Jesus as Saviour. The simple cry by those in Matthew's boat, 'Save us, Lord; we are perishing', is the prayer of the faithful disciple who knows Jesus as Emmanuel ('God-with-us') and Saviour.

Matthew generally follows Mark's gospel outline but adds a story about Jesus' birth (*Mt* 1-2), five major sections of Jesus' teaching (*Mt* 5-7; 10; 13; 18; 24:1-25:44) and expands the resurrection story (*Mt* 28). The last three verses of the Gospel (*Mt* 28:18-20) serve as a fitting conclusion and summary for the whole of *Matthew*:

> And Jesus came and said to them, 'All authority in heaven and on earth has been given to me. Go therefore and make disciples of all nations, baptising them in the name of the Father and of the Son and of the Holy Spirit, and teaching them to obey everything that I have commanded you. And remember, I am with you always, to the end of the age.' (*Mt* 28:18-20)

The *Gospel of Luke* is volume one of a two-volume work. The second is the *Acts of the Apostles*, the story of the first Christian communities and the missionary travels of Paul. The Gospel emphasises Jesus as the compassionate and generous host from God who dines with the socially outcast and rejected. Through Jesus, people discover a gracious and loving God, welcoming and inclusive of all of creation:

> Now all the tax collectors and sinners were coming near to listen to him [Jesus]. And the Pharisees and the scribes were grumbling and saying, 'This fellow welcomes sinners and eats with them.' (*Lk* 15:1-2)

Luke edits *Mark's Gospel* by beginning with stories about Jesus' birth and early childhood (*Lk* 1-3), expands Jesus' journey to Jerusalem (*Lk* 9:51-19:28) — which becomes the central place for teaching about discipleship — and adds to the resurrection story (*Lk* 24). The Gospel concludes with Jesus' ascension on the day of Easter (*Lk* 24:50-53).

The *Gospel according to John* was written towards the end of the first century CE, probably around 90-100 CE. *John*'s style is very different from the other three Gospels. The Gospel opens with a hymn which acts like an overture to the whole Gospel (*Jn* 1:1-18). It presents the reader with all the major themes that will be encountered in the rest of the Gospel:

> In the beginning was the Word, and the Word was with God, and the Word was God. He was in the beginning with God. All things came into being through him, and without him not one thing came into being. What has come into being in him was life, and the life was the light of all people. The light shines in the darkness, and the darkness did not overcome it. (*Jn* 1:1-5)

In the first half of the Gospel (*Jn* 1-12) Jesus performs what the evangelist calls 'signs'. He is presented as the Word, the living water, as the way, the truth and as the source of life and light. All these metaphors indicate the Gospel's unique portrait of Jesus. He appears more exalted in this Gospel than in the others. Jesus' exaltation and union with God is explored more fully in the second half of the Gospel — in the long farewell speeches of Jesus (*Jn* 14-17) that accompany his final gathering with his disciples when he washes their feet. Jesus' realised union with God is also evident in the stories of Jesus' death (*Jn* 18-19) and resurrection (*Jn* 20-21).

The four Gospels are an exceptional form of literature in the Second Testament. Each Gospel offers a unique portrait of Jesus. The Gospels invite us to experience him through the eyes of four different communities of believers distanced from us in time and culture, but united to us in our search for Jesus within the struggles of life we daily encounter.

For personal reflection or group study

1. Read one of the following gospel passages:
* *Matthew* 1:18-25 (An angel announces to Joseph the meaning of Mary's pregnancy);
* *Matthew* 8:5-13 (Jesus heals a centurion's slave);
* *Mark* 10:46-52 (Jesus heals a blind beggar);
* *Mark* 16:1-8 (Mark's story of Jesus' resurrection);
* *Luke* 24:1-11 (Luke's story of Jesus' resurrection);
* *John* 9:1-41 (Jesus heals a blind man — a drama of light and darkness).

2. Slowly read the selected passage in the light of this chapter and what has been said about the Gospels in general, and each particular Gospel.

3. What fresh insights does this appreciation bring to the reading of the gospel passage you chose?

Chapter 14

Letters

Of the twenty-seven writings in the Second Testament, twenty-one of these are epistles or letters. Sometimes a distinction is made between a letter and an epistle. The former is personal in tone and intended for a private, rather than a public audience. The latter is a careful, artistic piece of literature intended for a wider audience. Letters and epistles were popular literary forms of communication in the first century (CE) Greco-Roman world.

Paul used the letter to communicate with congregations that he had visited or was intending to visit. He especially used them to deal with pastoral problems that had arisen in these communities and come to his attention. Many Bible scholars suggest that of the thirteen letters attributed to Paul, seven are classified as 'genuine' letters from Paul, that is, they were written by Paul himself. These are *1 Thessalonians*, *Galatians*, *Philemon*, *1* and *2 Corinthians*, *Romans* and *Philippians*. The remaining letters were written by Paul's disciples, from communities that he founded. These churches dealt with new pastoral situations not addressed during Paul's lifetime. The letter writers interpreted Paul's mind for the new situation.

Paul's *Letter to Philemon* is a fine example of a Pauline letter and is one of the shortest writings in the Second Testament. In this personal letter to Philemon, the master of a slave called Onesimus, Paul writes on behalf of Onesimus who has run away from Philemon. Paul instructs Philemon to welcome back Onesimus as 'a beloved brother' (vs 16).

While the *Letter to Philemon* does not offer the depth of theological discussion contained in Paul's most famous letters, like *1 Corinthians*, *Galatians* or *Romans*, this letter is important for three reasons.

First, *Philemon* illustrates the fourfold structure that is typical in all of Paul's letters:

1. *Philemon* opens with a standard formula and greeting (vs 1-3).

2. It then moves into a thanksgiving section (vs 4-7).

3. This leads into the main part of the letter: the instruction or message (vs 8-20).

This section often has two parts:

One presents teaching on the Christian message (vs 8-14);

A second encourages the reader(s) to follow a specific way of life (vs 15-20).

4. The letter concludes with final instructions, a farewell and blessing (vs 21-25).

The second reason this letter is important is that it presents Paul's response to a pastoral situation. While the letter was personal and apparently dealt with the relationship within a particular household, the issue had ramifications for the local Christian community. Philemon was a well-off and esteemed Christian in the community (probably at Colossae in Asia Minor). Paul recognised that Philemon's response to Onesimus, also a Christian of the same community, would have wider implications for the relationships between other Christians of that same community, especially those between masters and slaves in Christian households.

Third, the principles that Paul used to encourage Philemon to welcome back Onesimus without penalty later became the basis for social transformation. The letter reflects Paul as a person of his own culture. There is no critique by Paul of the master/slave social structure; no hint of an attempt to abolish slavery. However, Paul moves the basis of the relationship between Philemon and Onesimus from one of master/slave to a relationship that is based on their being 'brothers' (v 16). They are united to one another because of their baptismal commitment to Jesus. This bond takes precedence over any other relationship constructed by society:

> Perhaps this is the reason he [Onesimus] was separated from you [Philemon] for a while, so that you might have him back forever, no longer as a slave but more than a slave, a beloved brother — especially to me but how much more to you, both in the flesh and in the Lord. So if you consider me your partner, welcome him as you would welcome me. (*Philem* vs 15-17)

Eventually, the baptismal solidarity between Christians became the basis for social transformation. So while Paul did not directly critique the social structure, he offered a principle that became the means of social renewal and ultimately led to the abolition of slavery.

Paul used the literary form of the letter to bring about healing in a divided relationship that had far-reaching consequences for the Christian community. That the Second Testament contains so many letters indicates their popularity among Christian communities as a literary form for expeditiously responding to urgent pastoral issues.

For personal reflection or group study

1. Read one of the following selections from a letter in the Second Testament:
* *Romans* 8:9-17 (Paul writes about the Christian's possession of the Spirit);
* *1 Corinthians* 11:17-34 (Paul addresses a serious problem over the gathering for the Lord's Supper in Corinth);

* *Galatians* 3:25-29 (Paul's famous statement of equality and inclusion in Christ through baptism);
* *Colossians* 1:15-20 (An early Christian hymn about Jesus, re-written by a disciple of Paul);
* *James* 1:1-11 (An early letter by a Christian leader urging wisdom in times of change);
* *1 Peter* 1:3-9 (A later first century CE letter; here the writer thanks God for Jesus and what he has done).

2. Slowly read your selected text in the light of this chapter and an appreciation of the Bible's letters.

3. What fresh insights does this appreciation bring to your selected reading?

Chapter 15

Apocalyptic Writings

Apocalyptic writing (or 'apocalypticism') in the Bible is one of the most challenging literary forms for contemporary readers to understand. Though challenging, it is not as difficult as it may seem. Apocalypticism was a special form of literature that existed between about 200 BCE and 150 CE. The book of *Daniel* in the First Testament and the book of *Revelation* (sometimes called the *Apocalypse*) in the Second Testament are its most famous examples.

In chapter 3, we reflected on the blueprint approach to reading the Bible. Those who use this approach and adopt a fundamentalist reading interpret apocalypticism literally. They read apocalypticism as though it is a literally accurate description of what is said and done. They read apocalyptic writing negatively — that is, as 'doom' writing; if a people do not obey God and believe literally what is written, then they will be punished as described in the writing.

Contrary to the doom interpretation of fundamentalists, apocalypticism was, in essence, a very optimistic form of literature. Its purpose was to encourage and reassure the Israelite people or the Christian community in the midst of suffering or persecution. Its clear theological message of hope was that God would be victorious over evil. Apocalypticism envisioned an alternative way of interpreting present history. It affirmed that God would never abandon the Israelite or Christian community. This conviction was communicated through Jewish symbols or poetic imagery. These images, familiar to the audience of the day, are unfamiliar to us and our very literal ways of reading. However, once the images, vision, auditions or symbols are understood and interpreted within each text's particular historical context, then the texts themselves take on fresh relevance for our own interpretation of contemporary world events.

The book of *Revelation* was written during a time of Roman persecution of Christians in Asia Minor by the Emperor Domitian (95-96 CE). The writer of *Revelation*, the seer John (*Rev* 1:4,9) — and not the writer of the *Gospel of John* — sought to help his fellow Christians reinterpret their persecution by the Roman authorities. He interpreted his readers' suffering by situating their experience within the broader context of Roman and world history.

In *Revelation* 13:1-4 we find John's poetic, symbolic reflection on this history. Here he interprets the Roman imperial power as 'a beast rising out of the sea':

> And I saw a beast rising out of the sea, having ten horns and seven heads; and on its horns were ten diadems, and on its heads were blasphemous names. (*Rev* 13:1)

The strength of Rome is represented by the number of the beast's heads, horns and diadems. The heads also represented each of the Roman Emperors. One of these was Nero who, according to legend, committed suicide and threatened to return at a later time to regain power over Rome's vassal states:

> One of its heads seemed to have received a deathblow, but its mortal wound had been healed. In amazement the whole earth followed the beast. (*Rev* 13:3)

Despite the historical situation and the persecution experienced by Christians, John, however, offered a message of hope. God would conquer and reign. The people of God would experience comfort and peace because God would dwell among the people:

Then I saw a new heaven and a new earth; for the first heaven and the first earth had passed away, and the sea was no more. And I saw the holy city, the new Jerusalem, coming down out of heaven from God, prepared as a bride adorned for her husband. And I heard a loud voice from the throne saying, 'See, the home of God is among mortals. ...' And the one who was seated on the throne said, 'See, I am making all things new.' (*Rev* 21:1-2,5)

This optimistic note which John sounds is a familiar one in apocalyptic literature. Rather than condemning the readers for their lack of faith (although a call to fidelity to God is always present), apocalypticism reflects a confidence in God's action in the world. The suffering experienced by God's faithful people is not the final word in history. In other words, the Bible's apocalyptic writing clearly acknowledges God's protection for suffering humanity. God makes all things new.

Fundamentalist Christians draw many of their ideas from the Bible's apocalyptic writing. They tend not to recognise the uniqueness of apocalypticism since they read it literally. This literal approach is similar to their interpretation of the *Genesis* creation story discussed in chapter 7.

Fundamentalists unwittingly gravitate towards apocalyptic literature. Writings like *Daniel* or *Revelation* use imagery that is amenable to manipulation by fundamentalists. The message which they derive from this imagery is one of doom and gloom for evildoers or lapsed Christians. Their teaching is always pessimistic. It is black and white in its moral teaching, with no areas of grey. This underlies the attraction which fundamentalism holds for many Christians. In times of social upheaval and uncertainty, people look for moral and doctrinal stability which can supply them with certainty. A fundamentalist reading of some of the apocalyptic literature in the Bible can appear to offer clearly defined guidelines for living.

Fundamentalists draw their teaching from the stark imagery and symbols of apocalyptic material, interpret it literally and then apply it uncritically to the present world situation. This situation, they argue, is prophesied by God in the Bible. They identify present global situations in apocalyptic imagery and symbols, particularly those from the book of *Revelation*.

Specifically, fundamentalists use apocalyptic material to uncover the divine chronology. This is the time line they consider God has drawn up, leading to the end of the world. This chronology is mysteriously implanted in the Bible. Fundamentalists argue that through careful interpretation it can be uncovered, the events of present world history can be measured against it, and the final cataclysm of the world determined. World events, like wars in the Middle East or the real possibility of a nuclear holocaust, come as no surprise and are part of God's plan. These have to take place in order that God's ultimate reign at the end of time can occur.

Such a blueprint approach to world history and social concerns has far-reaching consequences. If these events are interpreted as part of God's ordained plan leading to the imminent end of the world, then efforts for peace, reconciliation, the elimination of poverty or attempts to ease nuclear tension between nations have no real value. In fact, a fundamentalist approach suggests they could be considered as working against the order of history established by God. A literalist reading of apocalyptic literature in the Bible leads one to inaction or passivity to the world and a lack of concern about social problems and politics. Fundamentalism misunderstands the truth of the Bible, the subject of our next chapter.

For personal reflection or group study

1. Read one of the following apocalyptic texts:

* *Daniel* 7:9-14 (Daniel's apocalyptic vision of God and God's power, recorded not long before the Christian era);

* *Mark* 13:3-13 (Mark's Jesus encourages confidence in disciples who are suffering and know the pain of social unrest);

* *Revelation* 1:12-20 (The seer, John, has an apocalyptic vision of God and Jesus);

* *Revelation* 4:1-11 (John's vision of the heavenly worship of God);

* *Revelation* 18:1-10 (Babylon, the symbol of Rome, falls. All the manipulative powers that Rome uses are also crushed);

* *Revelation* 21:3-4 (A later first century CE letter; here the writer thanks God for Jesus and what he has done).

2. Slowly read your selected text in the light of this chapter and an appreciation of biblical apocalypticism.

3. What fresh insights does this appreciation bring to your selected reading?

Chapter 16

Is the Bible True?

A study of the various literary forms in the Bible raises a question concerning truth in the Bible. If we ask if something is true we are generally asking 'Is it *historically* true?' In other words, we are concerned with the historical accuracy of an event. If statements like 'Human beings have now landed on Mars' or 'A new cure for cancer has been discovered' are made, their truthfulness needs to be tested. These events would be verified by newspaper reports, eyewitnesses or scientific evidence. Such statements could be tested by observation, experience or scientific analysis. However, such truth — factual, historical or scientific — is only one kind of truth.

In Shakespeare's play, *Love's Labour's Lost*, one of the characters is described as a person who:

> ... hath never fed of the dainties that are bred in a book;
> he hath not eat paper, as it were; he hath not drunk ink:
> his intellect is not replenished; he is only an animal;
> only sensible in the duller parts. (*Act* 4, *Scene* 2)

In the context of the play, this description is not intended literally. The character referred to is not someone who is expected literally to feed off a book, eat paper or drink ink. Using poetic licence, the playwright is describing a psychological truth about one of the characters in the play who is illiterate. The statement is not intended as a truth applied factually to every human being living today, or as a historical truth about someone in the past, or as a scientific truth that can be verified by analysis. The play's poetic statement is true, though, from a particular perspective.

When I say that the sun sets, this is a true statement. Each evening I experience the sun disappearing beneath the earth's horizon. Scientifically speaking, however, we know that the sun does not set. What appears to be the sun 'setting' is the effect of the earth's daily rotation while it orbits annually around the sun. From the point of view of science, then, 'the sun sets' is *not* a true statement. From the particular viewpoint of my own experience and using poetic licence, the statement *is* true.

A statement or description hence can be regarded as truthful from a variety of perspectives. We know there is historical truth, but it is not the only form of truth. We have identified poetic, psychological, scientific and experiential truth. Though not mutually exclusive, they are not necessarily the same either. Poetic truth is not the same as scientific truth. To acknowledge that something is true, then, a distinction must be made between the *kinds* of 'truth' referred to.

To say that the Bible is true is a correct statement. But the truth we are talking about here is theological truth. Statements in the Bible may be based on a limited scientific viewpoint or understanding of history. Therefore they may not be true scientifically. Biblical truth is not scientific or historical truth. That is not to say that the events described in the Bible are not based on actual historical events. However, our preoccupation with accurate historical or scientific information is not the Bible's concern. The Bible, rather, is concerned with the communication of a true religious message or theological truth about God and God's relationship with humanity. This truth nourishes the reader's love of God. The Bible's truth is salvific truth. It is concerned about our ultimate union with God. Vatican II taught that this was the kind of truth contained in the Bible when it stated:

> ... [W]e must acknowledge that the books of Scripture, firmly, faithfully and without error, teach that truth

which God, for the sake of our salvation, wished to see confided to the sacred Scriptures. (*Dei Verbum*, n.11)

This book has explored some of the different kinds of literature found in the library of the Bible. The ways of journeying with the Bible offered in this book are based on the conviction that God speaks and reveals Godself to human beings within human forms. Literature is one such form. That God can communicate and reveal to us the religious dimension of our lives in such human ways is the basis for the important Christian teaching about the incarnation. God is revealed to us in the person of Jesus.

The writers of the Bible used all kinds of literature to express their conviction about God's fidelity to humanity, their experience of God's self-revelation and their overwhelming sense of being gratuitously loved by God. The styles of writing in which they chose to express these important truths 'for the sake of our salvation' were shaped by the forms of literary expression available to them at the time. Many of these forms are familiar to us today; others are not. One step in beginning the journey to read the Bible is an appreciation of the literary forms which the biblical writers chose to express important religious truths.

 For personal reflection or group study

1. Can you remember a time when you had a discussion over the meaning of a particular passage in the Bible?

2. What was the discussion about?

3. What was the kind of 'truth' being sought in that discussion?

4. How might this chapter help when people hold different interpretations over a passage's meaning?

Chapter 17

Continuing the Journey

There are several steps which we might take to continue our journey in reading the Bible and come to the kind of truth intended in the Bible. This book has presented a way of journeying that might be helpful to lead to that truth which is 'for our salvation'. I have indicated the variety of literary forms in the Bible, a brief example of each and the religious or theological message in each example. As mentioned from the beginning, this introduction to the Bible is not intended to be exhaustive. The following may help in following up some of the insights presented here. A first step would be to purchase or have access to a reliable English translation of the Bible:

Bibles:
The HarperCollins Study Bible with the Apocryphal/ Deuterocanonical Books. New York: HarperCollins Publishers, 1993. Uses the *New Revised Standard Version*, and is one of the best current English translations, with fine notes and detailed maps.

The New Oxford Annotated Bible with the Apocrypha: Expanded Edition. NY: Oxford, 1977. An earlier English translation of texts from their original language. The translation again is the *New Revised Standard Version*. The style is very literal, precise and most helpful for the student. It has useful notes and excellent maps.

The New Jerusalem Bible. New York: Doubleday, 1985. A translation based on the original biblical languages. Its style is less literal than *The New Oxford Annotated Bible*, however, its notes are very helpful. The earlier *Jerusalem*

Bible, translated into English from the French in the 1960s, has been the official liturgical text in the Australian Catholic Church for the past forty years.

The Catholic Study Bible: The New American Bible. Oxford: Oxford University Press, 1990. A fine translation with excellent accompanying notes and introductions to each of the Bible's writings by scholars of the Catholic Biblical Association of America.

The Jewish Study Bible. A. Berlin and Marc Zvi Brettler, editors. New York: Oxford University Press, 2004. An excellent translation, with literary, historical and theological information, tables, charts and glossary, by Jewish scholars. An important supplement to other Bible translations.

Introductions:

Paul Achtemeier, Joel Green, Marianne Thompson, *Introducing the New Testament: Its Literature and Theology.* Grand Rapids: William B. Eerdmans Publishing Company, 2001. A useful compendium to the major insights for reading Second Testament writings.

Bernhard Anderson, *The Living World of the Old Testament.* 4th Edition. Essex, UK: Longman, 1988. An excellent text for informing one's reading of the First Testament. The frequency of this book's reprinting attests to its popularity.

Don Benjamin, The *Old Testament Story: An Introduction with CD-ROM*. Minneapolis: Fortress Press, 2004. A historical and literary introduction to the Bible, with discussion questions, Web links and study resources.

Lawrence Boadt, *Reading the Old Testament: An Introduction.* New York: Paulist Press, 1984. This text, though dated, is difficult to better in its approach to guiding an introductory reader through the First Testament.

Marcus Borg, *Reading the Bible Again for the First Time: Taking the Bible Seriously but not Literally*. San Francisco: Harper Collins Publishers, 2001. This book from a fine scholar is an accessible guide to reading the Bible.

Raymond E. Brown, Joseph Fitzmyer and Roland Murphy (editors), *The New Jerome Biblical Commentary*. New Jersey: Prentice Hall, 1990. An excellent resource. It brings together in one book the work of some of the best biblical scholars in the English speaking world. Though a little dated now, it is still a fine commentary that covers all aspects of biblical scholarship and every book in the Bible in a way that makes solid biblical scholarship accessible to the non-professional.

Raymond E. Brown, *An Introduction to the New Testament*. New York: Doubleday, 1997. A first rate classical introduction to Second Testament literature by one of the best Roman Catholic biblical scholars.

Walter Brueggemann, *An Introduction to the Old Testament: The Canon and Christian Imagination*. Louisville, Ky: Westminster John Knox Press, 2003. A challenging and finely written overview of the First Testament.

John Drane, *Introducing the Old Testament*. Sydney: Lion Publishing, 2000. An accessible historical overview for reading the books of the Bible and is chock full of helpful background information.

Luke Timothy Johnson, *The Writings of the New Testament: An Interpretation*. Philadelphia: Fortress Press, 1986. A solid introduction to Second Testament writings. A worthy study companion for the bookshelf.

John Lanci, *Texts, Rocks, and Talk: Reclaiming Biblical Christianity to Counterimagine the World*. Collegeville: The Liturgical Press, 2002. An easy and challenging introduction to reading the Bible, with a particular focus on the *Song of Songs* and *1 Corinthians*.